the language
of dreams

poems by

cannon varnell

thanks to:

Ashley Edwards
and
Ashley Fletcher

for poetic ear

ISBN: 978-0-6151-4082--7

Cover art:
I Arise
by *Cannon Varnell*

to my muses:
Katrina,
Wendy, *and* **Mary Anne**

contents

union

fugue

mythos

disparity

union

To The Traveler
or
Back to Paradise by Eve

You who came through the tall grasses in search of me
With shiny black hair
Barely out of braids
You who sought the fruit of the vine
You who sought to make fires with his mind
You who ran through the fields catching butterfly souls
And called himself Traveler
In a hundred tongues
Who under wet, black earth
Tried to dig up his ancestors' bones
And in pool reflections
Tried to break the sky with stones
You who donned beggars' clothes
And withered away into pine combs
Who slept in prostitutes' temples and gamblers' homes
Whose heart burned like a choir of candles behind his eye
Whose desires led him to bed desperate lies
You who sat in the marketplace hungry, dirty, and alone
You whom the priests despised
Who spoke to lepers' wives and knelt at tombstones
Childless in dry times
You who discovered the science
Who studied the eternal spiral of climbing
Who reached out and put his hand in mine
Across winding rivers of shifting time
We finally made our way through the vines
On the scaly waves of snakes
Back
To Paradise

Suttee

I knew I loved you when I first tasted you
Like a fat blue raindrop on my tongue

I knew I loved you that first day
As I lay under the cypresses writing our wedding song

I knew when I could not hold a quiet light
When my angst burned brighter than the stars at night

I knew I loved you when my lips proffered my soul
I knew I loved you because I swam in your control

I knew I loved you when we sated the desire
When we shared honey and bread
For that first moon's length
As we danced around the carnal fire

I knew I loved you when the melody went higher
When the song became a dirge
And dressed in ashes
I placed you
Colder than my heart
On your funeral pyre

I knew
I knew
The moments told me so
I knew
A thousand years ago

Stars of November

A gray day sky
Stretched to late afternoon
Chris sitting beside me
Me in a quiet mood

Rusty leaves
On the sidewalks
Play chase
Swept along by invisible matrons' brooms
Contentment crystallizes in my eyes
A kaleidoscope colors his
In blues
An autumn day
When the stars of November
Shine
Through a faded watercolor muse

His black shoe, slick
On my doorstep later that night
Polished
Like him
Like his affection
Polished for me again tonight

As I pop the cork
From the top of a bottle
His hands
Pull up his woolen sweater
Unbutton his cotton collar
Moonshine lips
A prince's kiss
His aspect strikes the room
He shoots from the hip

A handful of hair pulls his face to my chest
A fever
A chill
Rough cheeks rub
Strong fingers caress
Drawn from safe alluvial terrain
With satyrs' hooves
We dance - dance hard and fast across the wild plains

His leg
Wraps round mine
The sheets and passion entwine
Shoulders spread
Blades unsheathed
We pound the primal drum

engram

my mind wanders
as it always does
to you
and your black hair
your almond eyes
flickering
across a thousand
arabian nights
from nowhere
a witty remark
you made years ago
strikes me once more
and like piano hammers
releases a chord epiphany
the memory
of your laughter
at my expense
draws a smile
to my lips
but not
you
to them

equinox

i pick the music
you grill two steaks at sunset
we buzz on red wine

cicadas chirping
barefoot backyard football game
twilight fading fast

quick breathless laughing
clutching your yellow shirttail
tackle in wet grass

you get mad at me
spray me with the water hose
i beg on my knees

you play your guitar
sing in spanish, something sad
i put the fire out

chewing on your ear
the hammock rocks us gently
we both drank too much

hairy ankles crossed
you lost your shoes in the hedge
just one sleeping bag

The Mystery

It is a mystery
that dark-haired man who
may love me

The mystery
rests in his hands
that without hesitation
grasp my ribs
and pull me near
to his silky heat
which naked rubs
the pulse
of my own hot heartbeat

The mystery
lives in his olive eyes
which turn
in any room
to me
close the gap
between all pleasantries
address my doubts
and confess a tenderness
hidden by independence

The mystery
lies in his bed
which toasty warm
calls to me
and with turned down sheets
and come hither satin
tells me I won't be leaving soon
that I'm a captive
in his room

It is a mystery
this brown-skinned man
who professes to love me
who daily says it
in coffee cups and back rubs
oil changes and bathtubs
who says it out loud too
but cannot understand
why I'm such a lonely man

MORE

There are more tears
Spilled over the years in the name of love
Than could fill an ocean or two
Mine alone could drown the world
Maybe yours too

At the time I was sure you were the one
So I unfurled my finest sails to pursue
But my heart asked
What's his name?
Love? Who?

I wanted a love that was more than love
But love eluded me
And so for the hope
For the sliver of a possibility
I held on to you as long as I could
Maybe one more night, maybe one more night
Maybe one more night before he leaves me

But alas poor fool with my diary of lore
I stand on the other side of unrequited love's shore
Wiser, older, less daring
But now more beautiful - stronger than before
I'd proven to God and Heaven above
That I had loved someone
I could handle more

Titan

His hairy knees
Like Pyrenees
Peak high above green sheets
Please my license
Ease me into longing
Invite climbing

Calm and pliant
Soaking in the balmy climate
His sweaty thighs lie open wide
Defenseless as I eye them

As if warned
The giant rumbles
The instant I pounce
He tenses and we tumble

Pinned to the mattress beneath
Massive elbows above his head
Massive hands trapped underneath
Fangs bared
I strike
Bite him and bite him

Until
Spent
The colossus yields
A Titan
And his tyrant astride him

Venus in Blue

Move your fingers
Around my breasts
Watch the chill rise
Aroused to your caress
Put your lips
On the nape of my neck
Softly, gently sensitive
Give me tenderness, finesse
Then kiss me somewhere unexpected next

Cup my belly
In your palm
Strained, pained, torturous
Keep your breathing calm
When my back arches
When my shoulders
Press against your chest
Inch lower
Explore
Touch the rest

Drawing the deep waters
Too close to the shore
Sliding on the sands seaward
I can't stand the current anymore
The waves crash around me
The spray is a blue bouquet
I fan into a million streams
And I'm crushed by the ocean's weight

anatomy

long
are the muscles that
wedge
down his back and
curve
to cup his butt
like giant hands
above thick legs
infested with
coarse curly hairs
that tease
from the ankles
all the way up
thick thighs
to merge...
you know where
which i imperceptibly
graze
on my way up
to rub
the furry stomach
feel the ribs quiver
shy nipples shiver
in bushy underarm laughs
that arch
his shoulders
cock the neck back
rough stubble patch
where his adam's apple bobs
giggling clenched jaws
because i
just
won't
stop

Mirage

Linger ever tender there
On the sweet idea
Of her smooth throat
Long-woven cloth at my finger's tip
Like the long-woven thoughts tucked away in my bag

My arms stretch to meet her across the sands
Across ages of grit
Seas of sweat
Stop the caravan
Let the camels drink
Let the concubines sleep
For this moon's length
Let me stay

"What took so long?" she asks
And the oldest fear is assuaged
But at long last, is she the One?
My mind hesitates
My heart wants to stay
Then let our robes fall away!
Free my mind and my body for this final reunion day!

Through dusty foreign lands have I toiled
Through desperate nights alone
This fever boiled
Across plains of dirt and sun have I come
In search of this lady
To be conjoined to this One

She lays her waxy palms on unarmored skin
Across my tattooed history
For this I'll muster all my glory
Let this be the end to my story
But she stares at me dumbly, flustered
"Is this what you seek?"

I make motion to speak
But my voice has grown cold
"Don't you know? Don't you know?"
She doesn't know what I seek
So I lay down beside her as she lulls me to sleep
To wake up tomorrow alone

waiting for a kiss

bathed in moonlight
the world is blue
like the bottle you hand me
as I rock on one leg
in the porch swing
dressed in your nightie
you glide back inside
turn on dave matthews
whose syncopated guitar chords
sing the story
and with the raindrops
provide a soundtrack
for this midnight afterglow

though you don't say a word
you tell me
in movements
that you're lost in former moments
panes of stained glass you
framed by spiderwebs
of a younger me

as many times as i have told it
i have never written it down
the story of us
how i, a barefoot poet
happened upon the philosopher queen
i wore blue jeans
sans shirt, sans shoes
and an occupied smile
ignorant of love and its rules
but hellbent on beguiling you
with my wily charms

you sat on a quad bench
chewing a number two's end
crossed legs, churning koans
peasant skirt and flip-flops
quoting nietzsche like an amateur
long red strands of hair
my blue eyes on your white teeth

those same lips
later on my forehead
upside down
me in an oak tree
in suspenders
feigning shy
and after the ball game
hiding in a hoodie
costumed possibility

your i love you notes
penned in mrs gorman's class
spread across my bed
as i composed my acoustic opus
which i finally played
the day kurt died
drunk off a single bottle
of snow creek berry wine
improvving incoherent poetry
because i was
young and drunk and twenty

you and me outside your dorm
after homecoming dance
on a porch swing
the attending rain
watching you inch closer to me
knowing what's to come
the same as now
waiting for a kiss

reverse rockabye

he wakes me
gently
reverse rockabye
so that i
pour
into his arms
alive
and grateful
for every beam of sunlight
streaming through half-lidded curtains

fluttering lashes
let loose my infant eyes
on toyland
in his scruffy grin
before
stretching
twisting
beneath him
i am a cat
with yellow yarn
in hanging tangles of fuzzy uneven elbows

warming
drawing him around me
in sheets
folds of him
smothering me
i am the sun
him, he is clouds i'm pushing outward
on blue canvas
striving to make rain

can't help but
curl
in the crook
his arm makes
wide
my hands are bicep bracelets
collars on mastiffs
growling
howling at my command

gasping
thrashing
grasping hold
choking on steam
crushed
in blankets of heat
i'm a wick dripping wax
he's bright iron
in a forge glowing orange

shuddering
exploding
flying apart
he is a comet
blazing
streaking through my galaxy
on fire
colliding with my furious star

untimely love

got to catch myself
before i fall
weightless shape
inside-out color
gyros and whirrs
whizzing past
platinum roses
starkly serene
but alone
nevertheless
ladyless
in surround sound
nights disheveled
whispering
dry lips
a wanton name
but
too afraid
to climb the mountain
brave the cave
crawl inside
open
to the exercise
willing
aware
halfway there
stumble, scramble
and catch myself
before i fall

Nocturne

My arms wrap
Around his shoulders
Wrists cross over his necklace clasp
Rough nape
Not like mine
His fingers tough
But smooth on my shoulders
And my stomach
Balm for a frayed mind

His scarred skin
Hides a hundred mended bones inside
Lungs expanded
Arms and chest wide
I run a finger down his back
Down his resolve and his pride
Then another sigh
A deep breath taken slow
Drinking joy-to-be-alive

When night eyes and starshine
And swirls of constellations hang high
Over my blanket and my story
To make a box to put my faith inside
Each star
A message from an older time
That this man and this moment
And this magical night
Are aligned so rarely
In a single lifetime

blue star

it is recorded
our love affair
in the nine intersecting stars
products of our kinetic relations
drawn in equations which reveal
our gravitational war

for billions of years
i've called you
in and out of revolutions
before and after supernovas
watching for you to make motion
come closer
to absolve me of my love for you

i was alone
in the dark
with no maps
no charts
no way to no home
just endless searching
through folds of night
and lonely clouds of dust

but for that love
my heart is cold
this ocean of space
the expanse we share
is the landscape of hope
you saved me
though you never knew
because i found you
i found you and you rescued me

and though eternity
will find us collapsed
surrendered to our own gravities
know
that your light
once reached out
and touched me
your soulmate
the blue star
at the other end of the galaxy

To Eve

I remember I met you in a garden
Illuminated by rays of light
Spilling through the trees
Your form, your voice
And immediate desire
Rose up from the dew to greet me

Take a step, I said
Touch my breast
Feel another breathe
Feel his heart and his chest heave

Come with me to my private place
A secret space in the green
Where I steal away
And where I take my imaginary playmates
To see my collections of dreams and animal names

So I took you
Your pale hand, your blue veins
Your small body
To a place that overlooked the sea
To a shady sacred grove
Of my father's forbidden fruit trees

And as the day grew brighter there
We basked in the sun, naked and bare
Until a hot cloud
Came rumbling through
And a veil fell between us
And *we both knew*

I remember thunder in the heart
Trembling in the soul
Undulation against the waves
The way tides roll
I remember lying there nervous
Friction, magnetism, and a spark

I remember an angry god
I remember tribulation
I remember the dark

Waiting

I lie in wait
Draped
Coyly naked across my bed

Inviting him inward
Writhing on my sheets
Writhing in my skin
Writhing in my head

Vials of oils opened
My perfume released into the wind
Swirling vibrations from my body
Rise
Give off heat
The musky smell of sin

Come rub my heel
Slither into my lair
Play double agent again
Where has he gone?
Where has he lingered so long?
I feel this mood drawing to an end

My waters grow tepid
My fires wane
The Devil won't come in
Though I blow hot wishes
Whisper secret fantasies
The guilt of need descends

Lust eludes my windowsill
My wantonness grows dim
My fertility
Proclivities denied
Perhaps I've called too often for him

fugue

Protest

You can arrest us
And chain us to your idea of beauty
But we'll persevere here
Fighting in the streets
For justice
And the glory of our own story

Attorney's Daydream

Leather sheathed
Legal brief
Hardwood floor
Tap-tap, beneath me
Silver letterknife
Engraved frame, photo of my wife
Wide-rimmed glasses
Ink blotter day
Ho-hum, a bottle full of rum
I'm wasting my life away

black shine

how old were you
when you tasted your first
cup of tragedy?
raggedy andy
forgotten in a corner
did the medication
turn you sour
or were you already green
frowning into your pabulum
before your lips
could even make the sound?

in adolescence
it fermented
into a permanent midnight mood
iridescent jet
grungeosie in broomstraw blond
gray eyes fixed in the distance
on some dire premonition

the shadow of some future doom
lay in a pool at your feet
so that you could
draw it upward into
a cloud of power
black shine
throw long shadows before you
all the arcane mystique
but without a story yet
to complete
the morbid nursery rhyme

it expanded as you aged
so that your electric
pulsing anti-glow
had a magnetic pull
that we could
hold between our fingers
like velveteen
pregnant with a deeper sadness
painful secret rage

as you approached
your darkest moment
that final unedited low
it became a shimmering veil
fluid and shifty
mercurial tar
so dense it was bright
and just as we thought you might
explode
you silenced
all your future poetic lines

it came as no surprise
that your red spraypaint cries
could not translate
gracefully
from scribbled angry notebook rhymes
into one more year
of strutting upon a stage
without some kind of compromise

for Kurt Cobain

the rules

i remember her best, hands clasped
on the edge of her bed
this woman whose prayers
must surely be answered
genuineness as a weapon
sometimes against me

then there was the cold one
in cotton nightdresses, swish, swirl
she had caught me again
without excuse
she could not see that i was special
the rules
did not apply to me

her demeanor, in which lay
no hypocrisy still amazes me
couldn't she be more selfish
paragon of virtue
southern mother bible baptist
to my open heresy

as i aged so did she
she grew wiser but still
could not help me
while i ate fire
she grew more remote
washed her hands
eschewed my misery
excommunicated from my love
i blamed her for the distance
and cut her off completely

but now i see her, dowdy housewife
not the empress of cruelty
she had given what she had
what else could she do?
i was special
the rules
did not apply to me

Main Street Melody

She wears big purple clogs
That lace to her hip
There's tons of glitter involved
Fake blue fur and a silver slip

She has a tattoo that shows
A kangaroo with a rose
That peeks through the fuzzy peepholes
Of her ragged fish-net pantyhose

She stands beneath my bedroom window
Making chitchat with the bar set
Stopping the frat boys on their way home
Bumming cigarette after cigarette

An occasional car-door slams to tell me she's returned
Back from a date, she'll have money to burn
She waits for Marcus in his Mercury circling near
If she's lucky she'll leave Main Street
And live another year

Sabrina's Breasts

Filmy translucent silk
Tucked into her belt
The pale stomach
The white peaks' pink points
Like alabaster
Like rounded porcelain fixtures
Like dough
The domes of jukeboxes in gin joints
Connecting a thought to an activity
Sabrina's breasts
Like nieces and nephews
Bounce across the room to greet me

princess of rehab

the yellow skin
flaked off her feet
around chipped ruby toenails
knees and arms
mottled with banana bruises
fingerprints pressed into her wrists
the eyes
amber flecked
cloudy jewel stones
haggard mop
of black strings
to frame the leather wrinkles
she was beyond sad
that stale flavor of sorrow
which no longer registers pain
the exhausted despair
of a tired child
who has already cried
all her tears
how many years
and what variety of abuses
could make a woman's
every word asthmatic whisper
fractured porcelain doll
toothless hag
princess of rehab

MAHOUT

I reach out
With my
Mind-eye-ear-word net
My fountain pen pauses
Accumulating
Little metal idea fish
Which I flatten out
In my metaphor forge
And slip into the gaps
Like a piano's black keys
Sensuous sentence trees
Erupt
With word leaves

Disemboweled thoughts
Tumble, rattle, sidle
Voices whisper
Some yell
Telling tales
Tragedy and ribaldry
Love, loss, and philosophy
Which I punctuate
With inky footprints
Across cotton paper
Invite verbal nonsense
Butcher American lit
Mad mahout
Riding atop rainbow elephants
A poet
Drunk on his rhymes

MISS HUNTER

Your curves trace mountain chains
Rise and fall
Misbehave
Your mouth speaks only Greek
Theta, lambda, function of x
I watch your parabolas slide
Miss Hunter
Do you think about sex?
Because I do
Do you think of me?
Your lips smack -- strawberry chapstick
Nude hose
Secrets exposed
Round rump
In a black glove dress
Beneath my desk
A boy's ideas
Grow complex
Could I be your man?
Would you dignify my request?
Or would you just arch your eyebrow
and pretend I don't exist?

for Yolanda

Come Dancing

Come dancing with me
The night's clear
Past the indigo twilight
There are stars as bright and far as you can see
Your mom said you're free
If I have you back by three
As if she'd check to see if you came home tonight at all

She trusts my company
Thinks I'm a wild boy
But secretly she wants me
Stares at my jeans
She knows I'm the good-hearted sort
Just the escort a girl needs
For a sport she played herself in younger days

All your friends'll be there
Manicures and warpaint
Braiding each other's hair
Gathered to chatter, laughing and smoking
Pockets full of matches and papers for rolling
Bright faces that squint in the light
Someone said Jack Daniel would be there tonight

You know that I'm right
You could use the festive air
A pause in that gnaw of your small-town despair
And I know you dyed a wild streak in your hair
So sow some oats with me Baby
Put on that red lipstick
And share

why i huff

i await that clank
pop
plop
shhhh
in my brain
as the drug
nestles snug
into my neocortical cracks
the buzz
i chase
into aerosol bags
existential masturbation
to escape
my crouching prison
of rage
the white shout
which i bleed out
rose petals
i'm a love whore now
starving for another kiss
from my chemical therapist
i'm a happy little boy again
flying high
on industrial string
panting
with bumper car glee
cuddled in the lines
of mom's spotless linoleum
lost in joseph campbell dreams
of bleeding vegetation
and carnivorous trees
i chew them
one by one
like iron guitar picks
chipping my teeth
soaking myself in rusty piss

eaten by laughter
my slave soul screams
getting fucked by life
and grateful for the vaseline

vieux carré

through the crescent city
in wet sandals i stroll
i am a firebird
in green, purple and gold
quoting j. alfred prufrock
to flies and mosquitoes
straddling the street
i'm the colossus of rhodes

i stop in a local saloon
drawn by its macho perfume
its lubed up inhabitants
mauve as mallows
work the room
it's balanchine clockwork
set to jazz tunes

chicken hawks and pool sharks
eye the wriggling fry
while guerrilla fashionistas
assassinate passers-by
ken dolls in tank tops
leave in double goodbyes
while the bartenders
slip in the storeroom
one by one getting high

i drink another hurricane
to preserve critical mass
alcoholic kool-aid
in a wasp-waisted glass
before i rejoin the street circus
glowing like brass
i stride for the door
and grab a black guy's ass

Babycakes

Why not catch a ride to my place
Babycakes
Come see the production Big Daddy makes
Feel my fat bed
Zebra-skin fake
To make you to sleep here
What else would it take?

Always flying outta the room
On your witch's broom
A kitty-kat collar and perfume like doom
Bound up in that character
That projection of you

Smile
Babycakes
Tell me I'm that strong one for you
Slick, sleek, sly
Wise on the fly
Hip to all your lies
A mind-lust-power tie

You think you own this town
Just cause all the toms chase you around
To get a whiff of your smooth, warm, wet, brown....
But like your frown - like your whole game
I ain't buying it
I know your name

And you sold me that same shit last week

for Kecia

Dream of an Empty Room

Dream you and I are in an empty room
Like Grandma's house
Chocolate on wood spoons
Her perfume
Or is it yours?
Like lilacs in the spring...
Like bees and breezes and bells
Dark forest dreams
Your smile melts in a Dali painting
Detached understanding comes
Seconds tick the time remaining
Your shiny face
Breathes my whole embrace
Draw back the bow
We watch the love grow
Like the rings of a tree
Concentrically
A glance my way
To electrify me

There's a glass vase
On a table in that bare room
And lilacs?
A white sheet?
No, it's you
Or rather, an archetype
But I lose you
In the dream
You're enmeshed in shades of scent
Flowery fragrance clouds my vision
No, they're definitely lilacs
And the petals spill into the wind

for Kecia, part 2

Disco Nun

Forms turn, stretch, swirl, and spin
Sleek shadow silhouettes cross through the room
Vibrating bass sends waves through our bodies
While electronic drums thump, bump and boom

Feeding the lust of the pagan mood
The Beast - the beat - strides through the room
In search of each other we converge here tonight
To gather, merge, commune

We chant the words
We call down night
Together, wet bodies
We move
Dark prophets forecast destiny
Spin webs of elusive clues

I spy a familiar moist back
Black spaghetti straps
Shoulders and arms raised
She bows to the dance god too
Panting, she stops, waits for the next track
Vestal virgin to apocalyptic groove

Amy

I've been after her
since the cradle
Her coy smile won't tell you
my side
how she stomped my sand castles
popped my balloons
stole every dime of lunch money
my mom ever gave me

She was always the husband
in our pretend games
which she directed from the daybed
Tarantino throwing pillows
Aghast at my performances
she often sent me home

She pinched
my cheeks, my arms
my butt
I was her slave boy
carrying her lunchbox
and purse and books
her diet coke for breakfast
Her majesty will now
enlighten us
on today's topic
of how everything and everybody
sucks

Older, she crashed my car
poisoned my goldfish
slept with Robert and Ian
but not me
copied my homework
belittled my manhood
made me pawn my TV
for weed

I lost her in college
to frat parties
library tomes
and a liberal arts degree
She moved to Boston
I married Sara
Annabella was born that spring

Ten years later
bribing the waiter
she's back
three wedding rings since
but still a divorcee
In five minutes she's
commandeered my glass
borrowed five bucks
and taken my car keys

Shindig

Hey crazy lady
Blonde wavy frizz
Mentholated leather-wearer
Drinking gin fizz

Sway the party my way
Christina Columbus come land on me
Start the aria over Darling
Take the time to talk with me

Pat me on the chest one more time
And it's a date I guess
You might go home with me
A warm tickly ride to my place
A blurry, blissful early-morning memory

Everyone makes room
As your sandpaper voice cuts through
You wanna slam tequila too?
Okay, we all say
And every twinkling Christmas light follows your cue

The snow outside's gone
Melted by you and your favorite song
We rock and sing
Swept up in your carnival-tent dream
Rude comments stopped short
So we can all share in your barroom sport
Entranced we watch you dance an Irish jig
We all vie for your eye
Red-nosed Rose
Queen of our winter shindig

Geisha Girl

What will I do
Now that there's nothing left to smoke
Nothing left to drink
Will the angst die too
My thoughts laid out for my guests
On an empty hostess tray
On a silver platter serving reflection
The geisha way
Bowing to the fashion of the next day
Come tomorrow
My roots will show
Come tomorrow
I'll have nothing left to say

When the party ends
When the last cork is thrown away
You'll find me sifting
Through the garbage cans
Looking for my mystery man
Some crumpled note, invisible ink
The one clue I missed
Elusive nexus of my fate

But I'll find my answer
No matter what it takes
If only in a single line
Because even if I don't find him
There's always the hope of next time
The party ends before the rabbi arrives
Everyone exits the room single-file
The minute we run out of wine

andy says pretend...

i'm luke skywalker
jedi pilot priest
you're leia in a bikini
leader of the rebel band
trina has mind-over-matter
and jordan, you be batman

against the evil empire
the blue sorceress
the lords of doom
freddie krueger, vlad the impaler
gargamel and azriel
the k.g.b. and fiends from hell
our many enemies surround us
orcs, klingons, the french
but we're fighting for the justice league
and those neverland orphan kids

hero of the apartment complex
flying windmill kicks
i can walk through mirrors
turn invisible
disappear and rematerialize
burn you with my heat-ray eyes
if you kill me i will rise
twice as strong
when i come back
i am one with the force
i can kill with a word
i am the kwisatz haderach

Lioness

Newborn with a fist clenched
She's got my attitude
Stubborn, headstrong, pissed
Child of some forgotten war
She'll take it on the chin
And raise her head up more

Brave, Lord, brave
Make me stay strong
Make me hold on to that noble young warrior inside her
Bless her black curls and brown eyes
Through trouble and death
Past the hard times

Should one so bright be mine?
Did I find a star to light my own path?
With charm and courage and pride
A lioness in a bassinet
Yawning in her sleep by my side

the ladder

at night
when all the adults are asleep
as her head
rests on a satin pillow
in pig-tailed knots
of rolled up socks
rung by rung
from the ceiling just above
descends
the magic ladder

a low whistle moans
the signal
and she's up! she's up!
in a whirr of sheets and bedskirts
her feet trounce the steps
over a bridge, through a tunnel
up a tree, under water
until she emerges
pristine in her party clothes
ready for *une belle fête*
in *grand jatte* seurat dots
petticoats and crumpets
like alice's party
and she's the hostess
toast to may day
with gingerale and strawberries
the guests are pirates and elves
princes and fairies
twittering into morning
bickering and gossiping
until a raucous clatter
sends her
careening down the ladder
her mom yells

wake up!
and she's up! she's up!
and she wanders to breakfast
leaving cake crumbs and teacups
behind in the creases
of her warm linen sheets

noblesse oblige

i want to be rich
every dollar is a ticket to be free
to require nothing from anyone
except the special attention
i may buy when necessary

no the rich don't need
what money can't buy
i'll make friends
among the artists and poets
i patronize

the catholics, the protestants
i'll endow with bestowal money
so that they broker salvation on my behalf
from the pews and pulpits each sunday

i'll build youth centers
for the abject impoverished hordes
health clinics
pawnshops
rehabs for junkies and whores

i'll hire doctors, acupuncturists
chiropractors and masseurs
whatever's in fashion
i'll pay extra for quick cures

food, clothing, shelter
love, health, respect
money can't buy happiness?
a poor person must have said that

Starclimbing

Arise boy! Arise!
But he doesn't move
Only his chest in cycles breathes
Deep in mysteries
He's exploring galaxies behind his eyes
In his dreams
He's a pilot and he's flying

His body is limp
But his mind is vibrant
Played hard with the boys all day
Now it's night
And he's unwinding
Not one more drop to give
He's lost in the heat lightning

I tousle his hair, but he doesn't care
So I leave to his comfy chair there
Admiral of the fleet
Deep in sleep
Starclimbing

for Charles

heaven shrugged

he sweated huge languid drops
coating the mattress and sheets in his earnest heat
his tears, twice as salty merged in streaks
around his bony cheeks as he called aloud
to saint francis who stood beside his bed, eyes aloft
as heaven shrugged

he moaned from his groin, groaned a mumbled prayer
half aware that he was pleading for his life
recounting wrongs back into childhood
which the saint already knew
as he humbly stood witness to the wretch's confession
waiting for him to discover his own lesson
compassion flowering freely, but lost on this youth

countless times earlier had he come to this room
the times the boy almost died
while courting romantic doom
with whiskey or mescaline, black tar heroin
splintering his mind with grandiose visions
trying to interpret what only left him broken

child of god no less than the stars
in his regard the saint made intercession
to this, as a hundred times before
he listened to the young man's wailings
his dire flailings and misguided insistence
that he was on a sacred mission
that there was another way
to heaven's door

mythos

the dark man

you remember the night of the parade
rain poured in sheets
on the slick streets
telltale rolls of thunder lumbered
to echo the lightning
the only lighting in the gloom
it was cold that night
you remember the night
that night that nobody saved me

i was pursued
through the back alleys
by the dark man
whose hands had those strange tattoos
like red jagged runes
my hem was soaked
my wet toes
hitting cold cobblestones
ached with the pace
but i ran faster

i never quite saw his face
but i could see the streaks
stains from the blood of a menagerie of sideshow freaks
around me
the smell of urine and glue cans

so i ran
though the tunnels
around the churches
but he hid among the towering spires
underneath the gargoyles' haunches
i was innocence
chased by rage
but the fear existed previous to this dark man and his mad parade

and that night
when it rained
as i ran though the innards of the town
the dark man
he caught me...
and he ripped my gown

since then
in the corridors of the labyrinth i survive
talking to my dark man
staying alive
i am a specter lurking through those same back streets now

since that night
you remember the night
when the city was black
while the rain swirled down the stairwells
that night when a revelation caught me
running through the streets
in my bridal gown

channeling

tingling
my arms and legs tighten
with an electric wave moan
arched feline stretching
tightening the skin of my brain
it arrives
as the sunshine dims
and the chirping of the coffeehouse
becomes a cardboard background scene
the paper people
shush
low goes all noise
cue the spotlight
for a voice over scene
straining to be still
my body hums
as do the windowpanes
in sympathy
like a wishbone tuning fork
overtones carry
like someone struck a gong
in a room full of drums
i try not to move
because if i shudder
even a millimeter
i'll unleash
ripple seizures
and soon i'll be an earthquake
of sound ripples
like the friction of a bass bow
the tune elongates into a single note
i crescendo
my pitch climbs
and a voice
from the other side

begins to speak
while around me
no one notices
staring into mocha lattes
that in broad daylight
in a starbucks
surrounded by people
i'm channeling

The Hanged Man

He wept bitterly
Until the valleys closed up in shrouds of darkness
And the flowers closed up in collars of blackness
And the Sun hid
And the Moon cried onto his feet

Her face
In every teardrop
Was strewn across the trees
The horses hung their necks and put their noses in the grass
And the wolves...the wolves bayed her name through the grey night
While his most secret shrieks
Ransacked the trees
Shook the trees

No morning came rising over the pools of his fatherland
No birds flew
The river stopped
Silent, it lay uncoiled and limp in its mud bed
And for the first night he had ever spent alone
The stars did not shine
No celestial light was available to him
Save the pale Moon
Hung above his pale head

The wolves bayed her name
And her face collected like gemstones in the trees
Alone
A purple iris stood between his eye and the night sky
Alone
It stared back at him
Amidst the flowers and the beasts

A purple iris stood alone in the wood
It amidst the moment
Gleamed
The word - the thought - was lodged in his throat
From the moment he ceased to breathe
In the morning the purple irises would come to bury her
In the morning
He would believe

The breath in his chest
Froze like his tears
Dawn never rose and never will
For him the moment never passes
The wolves bay her name through the trees
The Moon weeps
He hangs there still

FORBIDDEN FRUIT

I saw my mistake
Frozen
Watching clouds spin like ball gowns
When the world stopped and faded
Then crickets chirping and sunset colors swirling
Turned into angels weeping and demons shrieking
A starry sky spilled forth from the eastern horizon
A dragon crawled on his red belly into Paradise
Breathing fire and lies
While I cowered
A naked ape beneath the tree

AHASAMESUHSA
(ah-HASS-ah-meh-SOO-sah)

She was crumbling auburn leaves
But the trunks of trees
Were her insides
Lovers carved words on her
And the fairies called her Deacon

Her voice is now an echo
Of the mineral springs
Of the fireflies' dreams
Her only defense
Was the stickiness of her flowers

Call over the marsh beds for her
Whisper prayers to the streams
Gather red rocks and dress in reeds
Collect mussel shells
And wildflower seeds
For inbetween the evergreens
She still sings

for Barbara Gettle

69

VIBE

Do you like my vibe?
Wanna climb in my chariot?
Go for a carpet ride?
Are you hypnotized by my blue eyes?
Intrigued by the origin of my name?

Is it the vestments?
The jewelry?
The mystical jive?
No, it's the secrets
I possess
A glimmer in the third eye
That marks my tribe

My people are the burning bushes
Who shine through the physical plane
We carry the veiled lamps
Possess weird keys
Have maps
To the catacomb maze

We stay behind
Lighthouses over the rolling seas
Emissaries, Bodhisattvas
Masters are we

Darwin's Theory

A pound of flesh for an ounce of perfection
A gallon of death for a drop of fertility
Don't be mistaken, child
There's a purpose to the mystique
All the mothers bring their babies to me
Before the hyenas find them
And tear them apart for their meat

Promise nothing to animals
Their only sovereign is instinct
The truth is you should hide
Life is compromise
I teach them to survive
I am Darwin's theory

So give me a goodnight kiss
Lick the blood from my lips
Avert your eyes from the approaching fiends
And run to the forest if you want to stay alive
Run through the forest
But beware the trees

mermaid's dowry

eddy swirls tease
as the ocean laps the beach
threatening to cleave until death
drag me underneath
its whitewater dreadlocks

the stolid volcanic rocks
lie unmoved, black
like moribund seals
who need no longer navigate
the bounding waves
unlike me
whom the sea
seeks to grind like oyster shells
into iridescent shards

it will one day drown me
i am its maiden betrothed love
whom it awaits
to ravage like the ragged cliffs
with its water roils and mighty crashes
but not yet
i am still free
and my only dowry
is the time
i cheat it of its promised bride

horror

dampness and shade invade my room
from its corners the stormy night with lightning
seeks to penetrate my peaceful inner lair
not prone to fright i ignore the chill
of goosebumps as it seems the room
is eclipsed by a sinister mood
there is neither moon nor stars
i possess only candles which one by one
betray me in this darkest hour
i am stalked by paranoid insanity which suspects
that every cavity, cupboard, and door
hides an unseen horror
i wriggle away yet am captive
entangling in it more
i gasp for air, whisper stop to no one
almost groveling, begging for my soul
sensing apparitions are soon to appear
from the creeping night encroaching here
so to stay myself from flight
i light the candles again
but soon discover
it was a terrible mistake
that the darkness was my friend

nine eleven

i will pass into darkness
and pray for the light
through swirling rain
and the spraying sea

erect monuments
to the sadness of me
thin towers
with graceful steeples
to invite cataclysm

i seethe
in black blood
and hot sweat
radiating vertigo
lost in typhoons
my village is burned
and my voice
echoes back
ringing
loss, loss
like soulless bells

o death

o death
in liquid black
satin robes
with offal breath
and a voice that rasps
like turbine machinery

come in
old friend
my bag is packed
take me home with you
to the icy dignity
of your magnanimous marbled abode

i am waiting
panting
for your bony rap
on my bedroom door
i've put the seconols
in my blackberry merlot
ready for the ferryman
to take me to the summerland
where my wrists don't have scars
and i won't ever be alone

turtlerider

you were always the charming one
the poet with fair hair
the jokester
the fool
and I was your dolly sissy dear
the captain of the ship that loved you

you were born a freedom fighter
faery prince
turtlerider
but you turned down the crown
gave it up for the love
of her
that rumor of the wilderness
memory of elusiveness
mythic maiden
secret pearl
but she'd shatter like glass
if you found her
if you caught her
if you touched her fabergé world

she lives in mirrors
shadows of form
wily woman
beautiful and forlorn
in search of her reflection
weak from her scorn
somewhere along the way
you lost sight of the score
you get an arm's length
and nothing more

i don't know where your road goes
and I don't believe that you yourself know
why, oh why your goddess has forsaken you
but you can lay your head on my hip
weep a short while on my slip
take comfort in the folds of my gown
the way you used to
back before you fell in love
with a muse who refuses you

The Other One

These are desperate hours
Cross-legged sitting
Dragging my fag
Watching the smoke rings
Break in the stale air
As I go mad

My grief weeps for itself
In half-dreams
The moment
Cloaked in fear and relief
Seeps through the fabric of my escape
Like the blood swell
That's inching closer to me

Maybe I slept next to him too long
In the same bed
Same fevered womb
So close to the smell of death
To his gnarled flesh and acrid breath

His slimy lisp
His venomous hiss
The rivulets of hatred that twist down his back in blue sinews
That outline his hump
Slide around his sides and down his arms and wrists like snake tattoos

Shadow Twin
I banished him to the crypt
So that I took the brunt of his maliciousness
Heard every curse
Every hex that he spit

"I am in a constant state of evolution," the monster said
Skull leaned into my face
As I lay on a spiderweb
So that his whisper was more like a kiss
"I am legion," he laughed
"I can get us out of this."

Then his eyes grew dangerous and wide
As I watched his face switch and slide
And in a moment he had slipped through my grasp
To break all the china and ransack my house

I found him hiding
Cowering from a bright day and a mess to clean
The piles of broken pictures
Carpet stains
All the wreckage left behind
The carnage of the people who tried to love me

And as he scrambled vainly
His eyes never left the gun
You see, I could no longer be his keeper
So I shot
The Other One

The Fairy King, Part I

announced by not a single leaf
through the woods, you snuck
up to the footsteps of my temple ruins
unbidden but not unwelcome
to penetrate my isolation

overgrown with centuries of weeds and vines
entangled in thorny greens
knots of rosebush and creeping ivy
i was a wraith in reverie within
with no priestess, no pilgrims
to tend me in the darkness

as i wept in my cloister
past the cracked statues who pity no one
unnoticed by the living but not the dead
you crept
silent at my side, uninvited but undeterred
a fairy in a ghost story

absent opposition but not defenseless
i refused your charity without reply
as the honeysuckle odor
and the tinkling noise of your people
settled like scandalous locust
upon me and my sarcophagus abode

broken and stringy in wisps and tatters
my body shattered like window glass
my face wet with wailing tears
you laid me limp upon my crumbling altar
and as the crickets and nightingales do
i sang for you
subservient
as you poured out your mercy upon me

you cradled me
like a child, caressed my cheek
allowed me to carelessly weep
as you opened your flower bed
for me to sleep
dream a night in your orbit
riding on moonbeams and glowworms
in pearls of dew spray and star glitter
those nonsense visions of scruffy fauns and alabaster nymphs
of girls dressed in orchids and boys in buckskin breeches

i slept
privy to your mysteries
among your fairy kind who like naughty cherubim
flit back and forth in and out of the temple
while i nestled in your skin, purred like an infant
enchanted by the merry rattle
of you and your gay entourage

oracle

early
was I called
into the sisterhood
from the priestesses
back into prehistory
am I descended
the levantine oracles of old
keepers of the chalice
daughters of the mother goddess
I see the future
its branches, paths
divide and coalesce
roads which might have been
were
are
in parallels
cassandra mourning
I have ceased warning
the seekers I meet
about the nature of fate
chance encounters
coincidences
no one ever listens
to the simplest lessons
like packs of wild dogs
seized by hunger
do most men wander
through the forest
of human means
miss the opportunity
to transmute their nature
by the mysteries
into something greater
so I remain silent
about the seat of superstition

the cosmic message
found in a pomegranate
the same story in variation
fractal truth
in patterns repeating
the truth about destiny
that it
can be
rewritten

The Harpy

I know the crone you see
Haggard face and stringy hair
The green skin wrinkled by the ages
All talons and eyes
Death's stare

Can a harpy love?
Is she some beast squawking through the trees?
No
A harpy isn't a monster
But whom will you believe

Your father made me this way
Ask him who I am
Black horizon
Thundercloud
Dark Star
Ask him where my brothers and sisters are

I was born a harpy
Born to flap and shriek
A demon's life was dealt to me
My job is to cull the weak

A harpy can love
Love past her wrinkles and black teeth
Past the form and the image
Past the gulf that separates you and me

Know that I'm no monster
Inside me no evil beats
But know that I'm a god too
And even gods have to eat

TIME

i die and die
yet i exist
only the weed maidens
survive
my incessant onslaught
i am no rain
endless night
and dead seas
the bones
of ancient castles
upon ragged cliffs
i have quashed
all vision
and enticing fogs
with the suffocating absence of dreams
woven black
are the stymied hopes
of all things
even the sun concedes my victory
for i rule it
like all stars
i vanquish sorrow
and joy
i permit no immortality
i am the one god
you cannot worship
the end and beginning
of all things

banshee

she is a shade of the hills
mistress of the glen and swamp
druidess of these trees
shadow
who moves silently
through the cold air
until she wails
when the leaves curl in mourning
and her servants of fur
of wings and scales
lend a thousand voices
to her decree

dawn

there she climbs
glowing rose
the attainment of all her rhythms
synchronized
she has overtaken the sun and moon
in her cloak of blue
and jewelry of white cranes

in her lips
mix pinks and violet
that kiss the flowers
and bounce off the ocean foam
she dances in the distance
commanding the view
as i greet her on my knees
the high priest
of the mistress of the east
the goddess of the dew

Dervish

I am the dervish in the bushes
I am delirium in the vine
I am the hairy goatskin flask
Filled with red bloodwine

I am the eye of destruction
All that exists is the displacement of me
I am the rage behind the man behind the sword
I am the volcano's belly that seethes

I am the prophets' ferryman
As they pass across lakes of time
I am the tooth of the tiger
The mouth of the hydra
I am the brightest star that shines

I am the bud of war
I am the darkest seed
I am confusion
I am fear
I am hunger
I am energy

NEPTUNE

He comes to me when I sleep
Iridescent fingernails
Tiara of moons on my forehead
God of memory
Dreams
He comes to me in my bed at night
To lay hands on me
God of depth
God of myth
God of rivers and the seas
God who creates the other gods
Come again tonight for me

disrobing kali

she's streaking, peaking
uncontrollable indigo
seething cauldron
a thousand arms
electra empowered
enforcing karma
she disdains to descend
from the firmament
crop in hand
riding dragons
leading gargoyle armies
shredding heaven
mistress mayhem
bloody black
disrobing kali

the language of dreams

my bed is so soft
my thoughts are...
heavy, swollen
weight my head
pull me under green water
in my robe
plush quilt cushion
skin pillow down
below the surface
warm darkness
bubbling
indistinct mumbling
eases me low
to the muffled noises
interwoven voices
of flutes and bassoons
that flow to and fro
swish-swish, slowly sway
as familiar seaweed arms rock
and the soothing sirens sing
to invisible whales
clothed in black
who answer back
in the language of dreams

Miriam's Song

My brown skin
is a metaphor; it's dirt
My heart is a lion
My mind is an ocean
My feet are turnips
planted firmly in the earth

I am a wonder among flowers
a rare bloom
that which in violet and blue
imbues the starry night
with my ethereal perfume

I am a sentinel
I watch
I spy
through the holes of men's souls
where they hide
where they sleep
where they lie

I can see the horizon high
engulfed by my inevitable tide
If you're riding my ride
and I'll assume you are
then know this wave
is a tsunami
This flood could drown your world

I have drunk the gods' wine
swum in the sea's brine
borne the chiefs' disdainful stares
but all my shame is gone
I know right from wrong
I bear fruit
I bear truth
I don't care

I can cloak the valleys
in my umbra
shade the green, precipitate fecundity
push the seasons to change
make the lilies and orchids burst open
lift their flower petal veins
Watch as I call to the lightning
the thunder and the rain
Feel my tempest
Feel my fury
Feel my lust
and my pain

Old as the mountains
old as the sky
I stand before you to testify
that like my mother before me, in her tribe
the fishes of my sorrow
swim oceans inside
but when the day dawns
purple and wide
It's all in my palm
the World and the Sun
the Ocean, the Moon, and the Tide

for Maya Angelou

disparity

come back angel

come back angel
into the winding currents
of my wandering ways
make me an entertainer
set me free from my poverty

bestow upon me
your bread
which you sow freely
from the night sky
that makes farm boys into princes
even a boy like me

thank you angel
love
descending heavenly empathy
it's cold down here
where the rain drives
through the sleeve to the bone

empty endless walking dreams
vaunted cavity of desperate want
i drain
bleed
suffer for my wild ways

fly angel, fly
over the midnight canopy
of sad men's fantasies
dispensing hope
to beggars, addicts, and thieves
to all the people who don't deserve it
even a boy like me

Blacker Than You

I'm blacker than you
The blackest sight
Blacker than the belly of a cave at night
Blacker than a blackberry
Blacker than a panther's pelt
Blacker than tar
And blacker by far than a blackbelt
Blacker than you ever wanted to be
Blacker than the bottom of the deep dark sea

bored with hell

weary
and meek
do i come
humble
to the house of pain
in my iron shackles
stretched
to supplicate to my sad master
who is always the first to scream
so tired
of the whip, bored with my chains
all day in the stocks
i wander away

Those Eternal Ones of the Dream

the petrified strata
backward into prehistory
layer upon layer
through striations
of dust gone rock
tinted with blood
red, blue, yellow
with frond prints, shell reliefs
and the seeds of proto-fauna
so elegantly
the story tell
of the world bloom
which precedes us --
the flowering
of reptilian memory
progressed
through animal brains
the ancestors of us all
those eternal ones of the dream

end of the line

i have come to the end of the line
where i live or die
before the black volcanic rocks
where the wild hibiscus
blooms haphazard scarlet
before the horizon shadows
of waltzing sailboats
and cruise ship lights
jewelry against the sky so rose
the harbor is alive
somnambulant in civil twilight
like my darker selves
in candled requiem
softly night invoking

by drowning, noose, or cliff
what would kill me quick
or will something stop me still
gleaming knight on a horse in white
or a browned wisewoman's
clucking scold
or
no one
not another soul
to hinder or deter
the consummation of my sad pavane

shall i lay
pale petals
for wind dispersal
let fly my paper bones
over the fat waves
dazed
scatter me like chum
dissolution back
into subconscious soup
surrender to surrender
and cut the tether
fade
from black
into blue

freedom song

today is my freedom song
wherein the sun with glorious love
and tender sentiments
meets me halfway
through the dawning sky
surrounded by love letters
composed by morning birds
i awake with grassy ideas
and greet cloud sculptures
which enfold my heart
instill a longing for the playful winds
which ignite the embers
of yesterday's passions
and breathe the restful promise
of the dreams of today
when all the chorus
the rocks and the sea
the beasts and the flowers
like me
wave in anthems high
because today is my freedom song

for Kahlil Gibran

Dear God

Dear God
This letter is just like before
A plea for a pardon
And a request for more

I agreed to work for you in a distant past
But as the days pass
As my mind is worn
I can't grasp
Can't quite recall
What it was I started this war for

A Word from the Almighty

I didn't ask for this God thing
I didn't know what I was making
Just playing with clay
It was all an experiment

You think I got it easy?
Well, I've gone crazy
In the spillions of years
That I've been here alone

Sorry, kids
You're on your own

Don't ask me about salvation
Evolution is natural
If you knew what I knew
You'd shut up and sit down

Matter is energy
Is time is space
Is everything
All things are necessary
There's no way to err

So save your bloody offerings
I *don't* want your virginity
Every use of my name
Is sacred and vain
Because I couldn't care less
What you do

Take it from the revelator
It's all up to you

mountainclimbing

the white clouds loll above
in slopes of smoke the furry wisps pass
like a projector casts images on a blank screen
shadows shined on the ceiling of our pup tent
pitched over the tops of the trees

hawks loop feathertips through the sky
the altitude breathes a sting
as winter trickles down the mountainside
the earth is dark and the wind is cruel
but the sun shines

palette drawn from the leaves
we see the seed queen mourn the spring
the breeze whispers loss in our ears
but our hopes ride on dragonfly wings

the feel on our skin
of sunshine arms that extend
in a firm and solid embrace to the sod
to the grassblades that tickle us
as we sit on the mountaintop

souvenir rock in my pocket
i stand to spy the valley beneath
a man manifests where a dream once stood
glimmer of light through the trees

free of voices

her words replay often in my head
my mother's voice
ever since i began this journey
we must take chances
far away from childhood
she calls my name
through layers of sleep
stilling the moment
as i tread a foreign street
there are few traces
of my origin left
i have passed
into far too distant lands
in search of me
almost far enough
to discern myself free
free of voices
free of the voices
that remind me i'm dreaming

Fallen

All my words are angry
Every song grates against my bones
The sun scorches
The air is putrid, sweet
My mouth is dry
My calves ache
I don't remember where I come from
Where I'm going
I have no beliefs
I am a punishment manifest
For sins I don't remember
Can find no shelter
No rest for my swollen feet
I'm wandering, wandering
Far away from heaven
Can you tell me
Where the other angels sleep

drops

the drizzle goes
and the drops grow
fed by every touch
and each one makes a rainbow

sad days
like these
i know
the gray-blue attitude
reflective soul
streams of thought, of consciousness
roll

i don't mind the feeling
the cold in my bones
the downward spiral
of cosmic martyr syndrome

when my teeth chatter
when the poems get sadder
the hollow gets louder
and the fantasy shatters

nothing matters

but the drizzle goes
and the drops grow
fed by everything they touch
and each one is a rainbow

our lady

ecce ancilla domini
once
alone
in the cathedral of chartres
she spoke to me

our lady of the sorrows
of the mysteries
of compassion and mercy
love
she said
is the greatest of these

i was a sobbing child
transfixed
by her humanity
i fell to my knees
weeping at her words
for with those words
she
changed me

between the mountains
and the sea

between the mountains
and the sea
sits all of me
my totality
so that even the air i breathe
carries the brackish scent
of my self-indulgent reverie
i move unevenly
roll over
arms and legs and head
untangling deliberately
medusa mop
of lazy snakes
uncoiling memories
that multiply
and eclipse the day
in an infinite daydream
of ever-budding clarity
unraveling regrets here
where i set my ghosts free
to confront and accuse me
where wounded and penitent
i silently grieve
on this lonely, crowded beach
between the mountains
and the sea

holy man

i am
tattered robes
of gray and brown me
rolling along the asphalt
dawning city, shiny and cold
the night is passing
along with my identity
from alley prowler
to don of downtown
combing the gutters
for quarters and coffee

self-proclaimed scholar
pilgrim to the holy city
tattooed sadhu
beneath beard and big coat
whom you'd ignore
at the gas station or on the street
whom the propaganda failed to reach
who's searching for god
in a literal way
hunger is my employer
life is my teacher
i am free
to borrow from buddha or black elk or star wars

i am a holy man
though invisible
studying poverty
i wish i could reach you
there inside your s u v
comfort you, teach you
release you from your suffering
but why should you listen to me?
i'm just some homeless man
who sleeps at the salvation army

for all the men at IHS in Honolulu

Kind Sir

Kind Sir
You have caught me
Pants down
At the start of Armageddon
Yes I heard about the earthquakes
And hurricanes
I thought it was just bad weather
Who knew?
Oh right, you did

Well forgive me
As I am not a member of the holy host
I apologize again
Perhaps if you
Could have spared
An emissary in the last few years
I wouldn't be here
Unawares
Without blessed rubbers
In the ash and brimstone rain

I am mortal after all
Unconnected to
The worldwide psychic web
Except in dreams
But who pays heed to dreams?
Oh right, you do

So apparently it's Doomsday
I've packed a bag
Dumped all my currency
Back to the Stone Age we go
No need for a change of clothes

The party's over
The bill's come due
You've come calling
And it seems I've stepped on some toes
So for all the saints I profaned
And all the virgins
I wooed
I confess

I did believe in the messiah too
But where was he
In the intervening years
When we needed him
Here
To save us?

For all my zealous professions
Midnight declarations
Theological protestations
All I have to say is
They were every one
Earnest words

If I sound without faith
It's true
I had no piece to build upon
Ever since I was left behind
Without bodyguard
Without ally
Or even equal foe

Was that the test?
To see how I handled everything
While stuck here completely alone?
Well, kind Sir
That's fucked up
See: page 19 of my note

SACRAMENT

Bless this, Lord
Sacrament
Holiest of grapes
Visionary magic water
Take my pain away

I came today
To say a prayer for You
That You're watching and You're real
Great Cosmic Spirit Womb
Me, I ride the Möbius strips
Inside Your belly's blue balloon

And maybe some other time
I could join Your chorus line
When red velvet lust drapes
Don't flutter in my mind

Bless You Father
And Your purple juice
Sorry I got drunk on the temple wine
I won't bother with an excuse

Thank You Livingston

hopeful stars

do you remember our young days?
never forget the promises we made
that the little dewdrop seeds
of our early dreams would someday manifest
translate our oblivious delight at life
from mere curiosity and need
into a twinkling
gold and silver sea
of a trillion hopeful stars

discerning the priesthood

when i think
of how much incense
burned to remedy
the lives ruined
broken trust
dropsy cures
and snake oil potions
cannot treat
the flaming ego-itis
lit like guilty wicks
fire licking
the naughty lips
that swear like pig sailors
at sorceresses
impotent threats
blaming kisses
upon the foreheads
of sacrificial children
as they're tossed
into the pit
of the feathered god
who would not be named
lest his observants
uncover his naked shame
and unleash
upon the world
a misery box
of ignorant clues
that lead a path back
to former cave conspiracies
where our ancestors rotted
in the name
of mutilated purity
smoking doctrine

that the shamans gleaned
but fed the carcinogens
of clergy's needs
until the creed
became a guilt prison
of genuflecting deceit
and the virgins
were no longer free
to walk away

to the one god: regarding my resignation

to you
moby of lords
holder of the star colander
artist of the first canvas
juggler of mighty rocks
i hereby resign
give up
will try no more
am not interested
in any leadership positions

priapus amid muses
mother of invention
zen temple hermit
slayer of the aryan gods
i find
that everything
outside
the shelter you provide
only yields blossoms
of white blister misery for me

mystic anti-theist shapeshifter
chaos theologian
chairman of the first cabal
protector of the lunatic fringe
you have tipped your hand
i lose, you win
no contest
my megalomania
has reached its inevitable end
have mercy on a fool

jovial patron of centrists
primary referent of curses
benevolent chief philanthropist
shepherd of sly schmendricks
the remainder of my earthly time
i yield
to you
the one god

PSALM

I am a servant to my Master
To my Maker -- to my God
Sinews fashioned by His hands
I was molded to be strong

I stretch my arms to embrace His world
Stand tall to face the Sun
I smell the flowers as they unfurl
I hear the rivers run

I stamp my feet upon the earth
I dance into the wind
I nourish my body with many fruits
My solace I find in Him

In the storm's wake I stand fast
Tent stakes planted firmly in the grass
Bare-chested and bare-footed
Barely humming and strumming my strings
Offering the age-old hymns
Until He joins me as I sing

for my mother

Prayer To The Yellow Angel

Sunshine all day
Bubblebath at its finish
Some awesome, starstruck Romeo
A fridge full of feta and spinach

Pasta and tomatoes
Bread and cheese
A billowy bedspread in my air-conditioned home
Water music to soothe me

Palettes of paints
Metal scraps and solder
Americans at The World Cup
Kind memories of my father

Books in Greek, Latin, Chinese
The power to punish mean people
Being awake inside my dreams

Plane tickets to Lhasa, Accra, and Taipei
E-mail from my inner circle
Herb teas to sample each day

A tree-lined lake
Visible from my bedroom window
Arms, shoulders, a corvette
Plans for tomorrow

unwilling

i don't know
when it began
this love affair with death
perhaps I coalesced
in the womb this way
saturated by blackness
unwilling

gaunt and sad child
sweating blood droplets
alone and palely loitering
for some *belle dame*
bête noire monster lover
to come and dracula me dry
demoness paramour
to personify my suicide

did I choose
to live out these fantasies
of the darkest plumes in eternity
of winged night courting me?
do i advertise untimely demise?
is my soul truly black?
do all things living
despise me back?
gladly usher me
toward the grave?

grateful

for every drop of rain
on us dry creosotes
a warm shower
and donated clothes
cool grass on hot nights
a bed if not a home

soup kitchens that smell like bread
seconds at supper
supper at all
the tools of agriculture
to nourish the seed
and me

children
all trees
for every flower blooming
and red birds
for music -
the reed and the string
piccolos
and kettledrums
for what they sing to me

grown men who whistle
doting old ladies
who take in strays
and derelict hippies
who on quiet roads
share lonely crusts of bread

for the violet sky
wherein fly yellow moons
that drip sticky poetry
those rowdy words
rioting in my head
which with ten-for-a-dollar pens
put to blank paper
my gratitude

the poet

Cannon Varnell was born in 1974
in southern Arkansas.
He attended the University of Arkansas
in Little Rock where he studied
anthropology, sociology, and
linguistics, but not poetry.
In 2004 he moved to the island
of Maui where he now lives.
This is his first book.